Music Students Have Higher Test Scores!

Six Later-Elementary Level Piano Solos

Splattered With Style!

by

Glenda Austin

Contents

12161

For Max Cassilly

Chuggin' Along

Animated!

Glenda Austin

Slow down.
Gradually accelerate.
L.H.

Irish Morn

Glenda Austin

Spirited

Coda
f
p
rit.
softly
a tempo
poco rit.

Oriental Spring

With feeling and not hurried

Glenda Austin

L.H.
p
L.H.
mf
mp
linger
fade to the end
8va
pp

For Sarah Elizabeth Austin

Black Cat Bounce

Glenda Austin

D.S. al Coda
Coda

For Meri Rogers

Mexican Celebration

Glenda Austin

f
f
mf
f

12161

"O - le!"

For Matthew Holt

On the Right Track

Glenda Austin

On D.S. do not repeat,
but go to Coda.
D.S. (without repeat)
al Coda

Coda
p
sfz
p
sfz
p
sfz
f
f
f
sfz